WHEN I'm ANGRY

written and illustrated
by
JANE AARON

Golden Books
NEW YORK

Golden Books®

888 Seventh Avenue
New York, NY 10106

Copyright © 1998 by Jane Aaron

Golden Books® and colophon are trademarks of
Golden Books Publishing Co., Inc.

Designed by Gwen Petruska Gürkan

Manufactured in the United States of America

10 9 8 7 6 5 4 3 2 1

Library of Congress Cataloging-in-Publication Data
Aaron, Jane.
     When I'm angry / written and illustrated by Jane Aaron.
           p.   cm. — (The language of parenting : 2)
     "A parent's guide to anger by Barbara Gardiner" : p.
     Summary: Explains anger as a normal part of life and discusses how
to deal with it. Includes a parent's guide in a question-and-answer
 format with examples and suggestions.
     ISBN 0-307-44019-2 (hardcover : alk. paper)
     1. Anger in children—Juvenile literature.   2. Parenting.
     [1. Anger.]   I. Gardiner, Barbara. Parent's guide to anger.
     II. Title.   III. Series.
     BF723.A4A27   1998
     152.4'7—dc21   98-12721
                          CIP   AC

For Sam and Florence, with love.

SOMETIMES I'm SO ANGRY

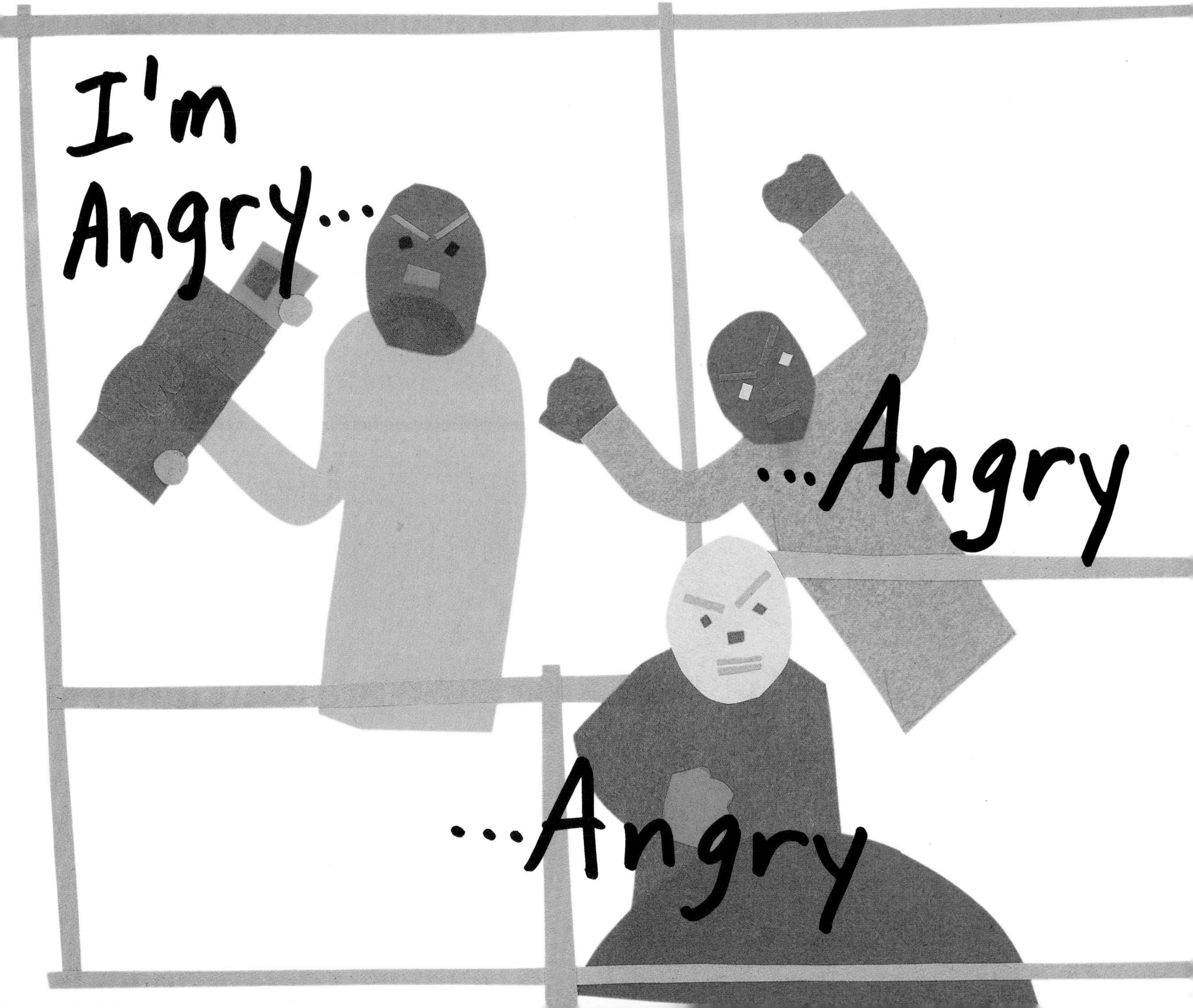
I'm Angry...
...Angry
...Angry

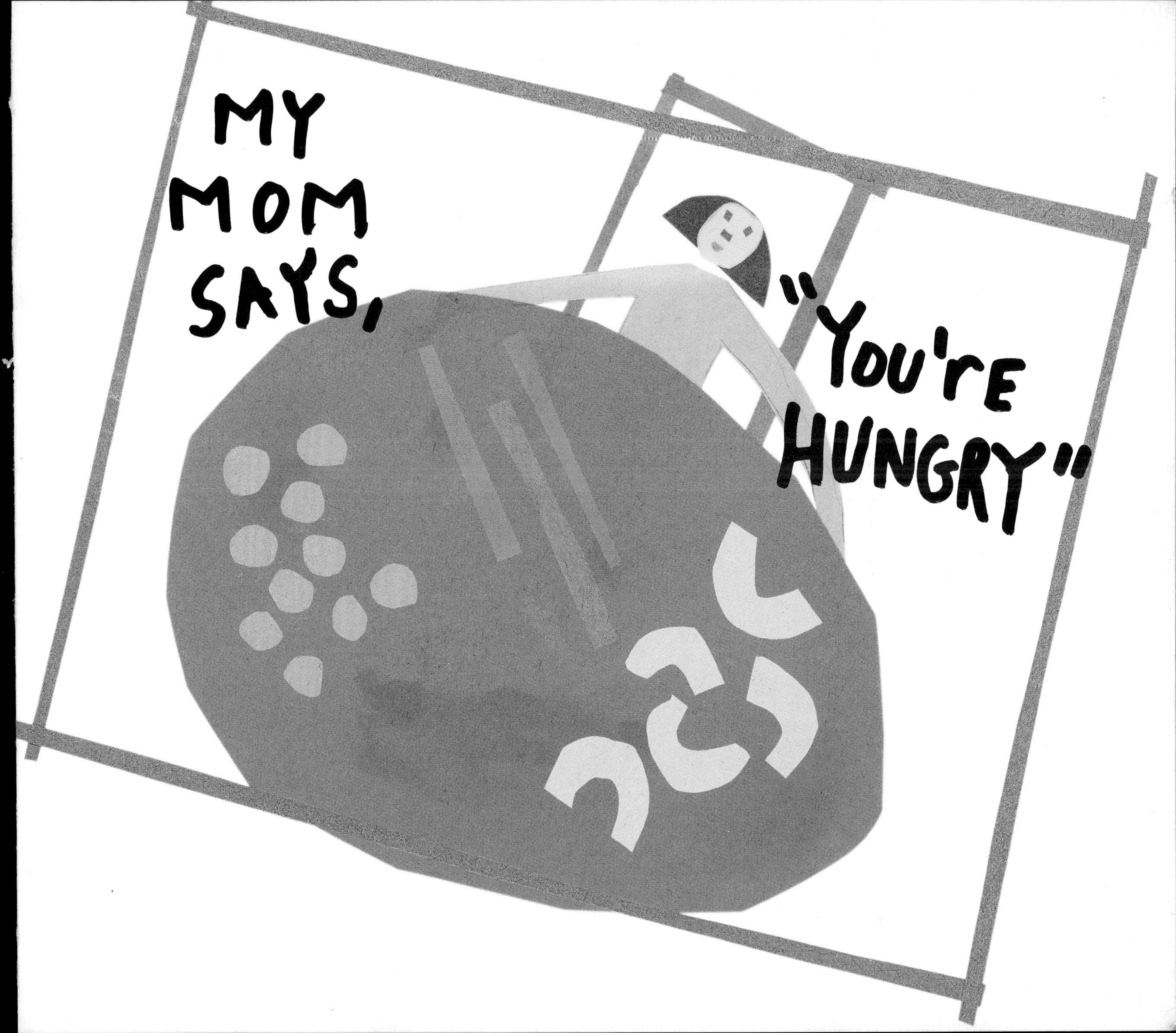
MY MOM SAYS,
"YOU'RE HUNGRY"

I
AM
NOT

MY
DAD SAYS,

"YOU'RE
TIRED"

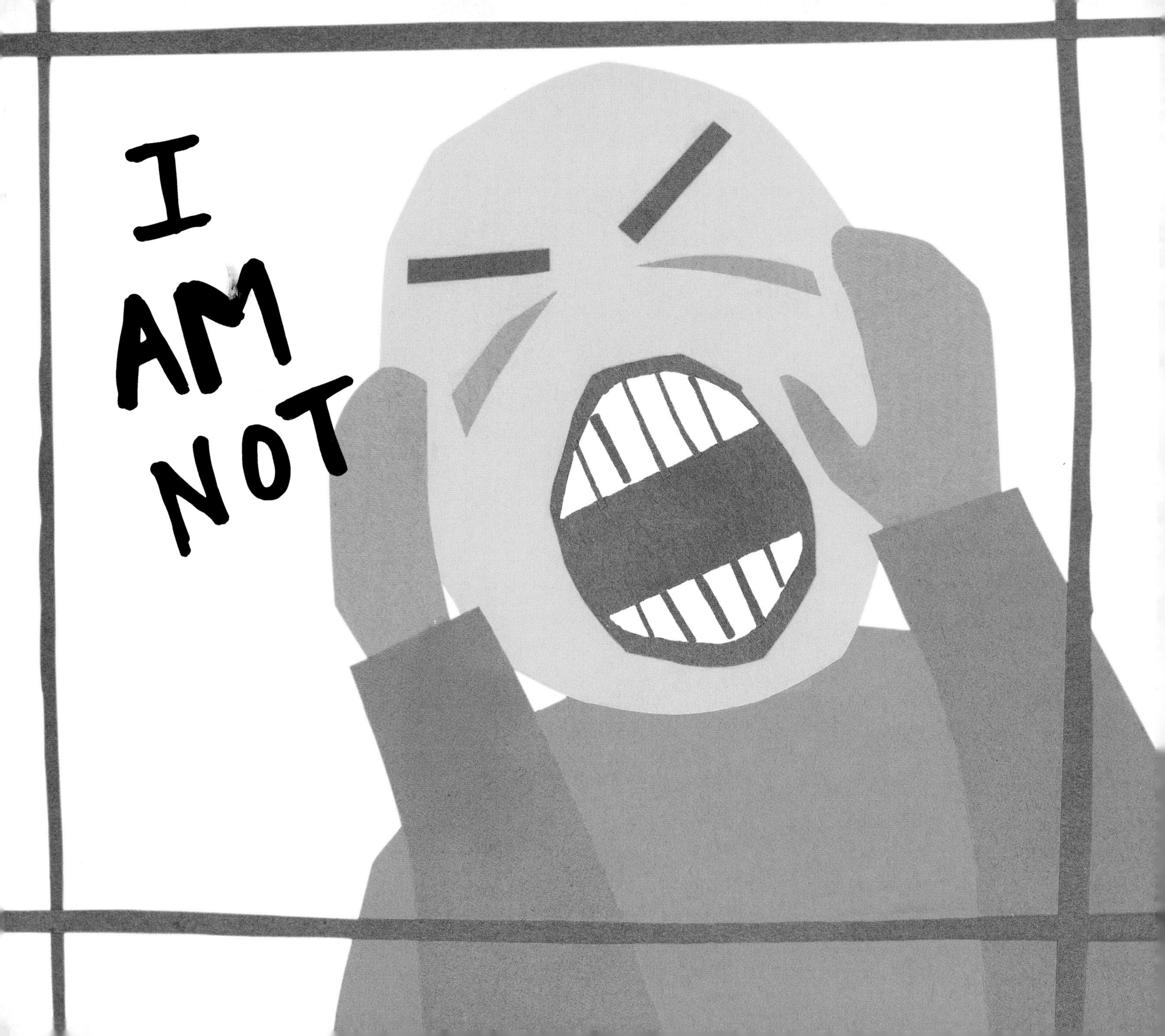
I AM NOT

I'm just

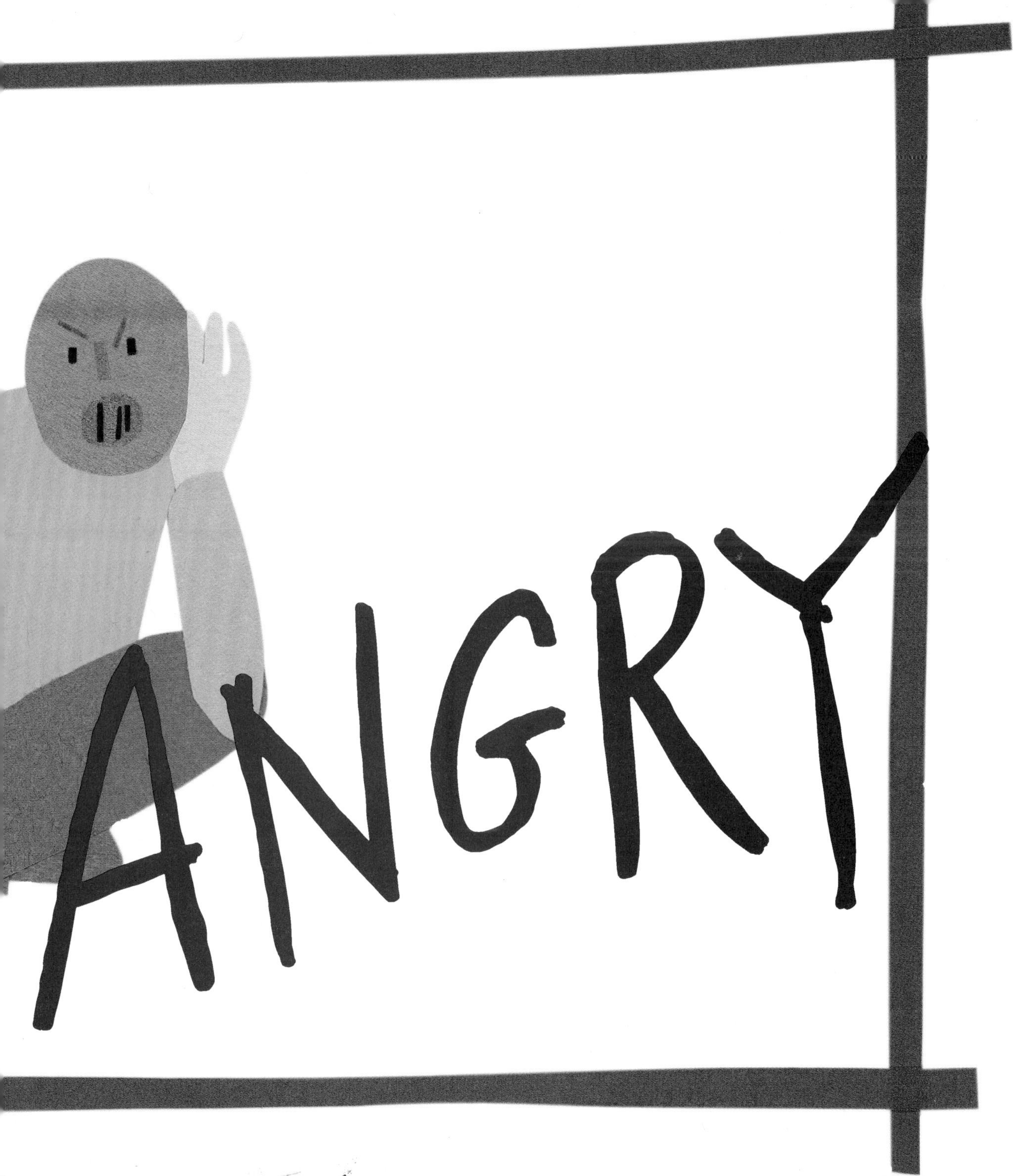
ANGRY

and
IMPORTANT

OR SHOUTING MEAN WORDS

SOMETIMES
I FEEL LIKE
NOBODY
is LISTENING

OTHER TIMES BEING ANGRY MAKES ME WANT TO CRY

and
I want
to
STOP

SO I talk to my MOM and tell her how I feel

OR I LET MY TOYS DO THE SHOUTING

Sometimes I want to be by myself for a while

IT'S OKAY TO BE ANGRY SOMETIMES